The Warm-Blooded Dinosaurs

Library of Congress Cataloging in Publication Data

May, Julian.
  The warm-blooded dinosaurs.

  Includes index.
  SUMMARY: A simple discussion of new evidence
that dinosaurs were warm-blooded animals and not
reptiles as previously believed.
  1. Dinosauria—Juvenile literature. 2. Body
temperature—Juvenile literature. [1. Dinosaurs.
2. Body temperature] I. Bjorklund, Lorence F.
II. Title.
QE862.D5M38   568′.1   77-24642
ISBN 0-8234-0312-2

JULIAN MAY

The Warm-Blooded Dinosaurs

drawings by LORENCE F. BJORKLUND

HOLIDAY HOUSE · NEW YORK

Dinosaurs lived long ago.
And dinosaurs are gone.
Most people are sorry about that.
We would all like to see a living dinosaur.
A zoo of dinosaurs would be
the most wonderful zoo in the world.

But dinosaurs are long gone.
Scientists tell us that the last ones
died about sixty million years ago.
All we can see today are their fossils—
bones and footprints
that have mostly turned to stone—and
models that scientists hope are correct.

We cannot see a living dinosaur.
But some animals of today look a little
as dinosaurs must have looked.

KOMODO DRAGON LIZARD
about 3 meters (10 feet) long

FLORIDA CROCODILE
about 4½ meters (15 feet) long

8

NEW ZEALAND SPHENODON (TUATARA)
about 60 centimeters (2 feet) long

These are all cold-blooded reptiles—
their bodies are as cool as the air around them.
Are they close relatives of dinosaurs?

MEXICAN IGUANA
about 1½ meters (5 feet) long

9

Scientists say "No."
None of these animals
is a close dinosaur relative.
Here is a family tree
of animals with backbones.
It shows that dinosaurs suddenly
disappeared from the earth.
It seems they had no close modern relatives.

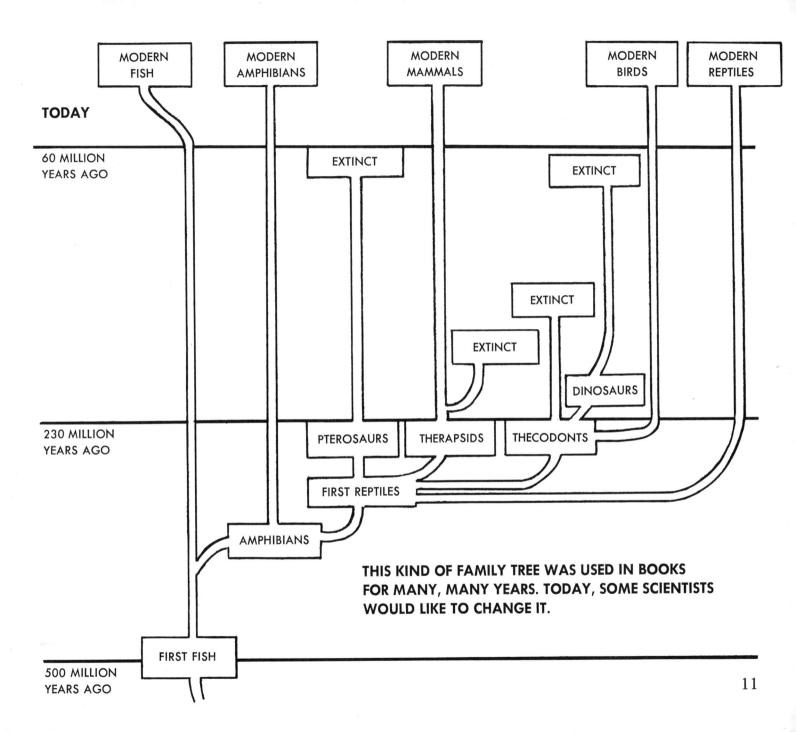

11

Children who go to museums
and read dinosaur books love dinosaurs.
But most scientists don't.
Scientists say, "Dinosaurs long ago came to an end.
We'll study animals that were a real success."

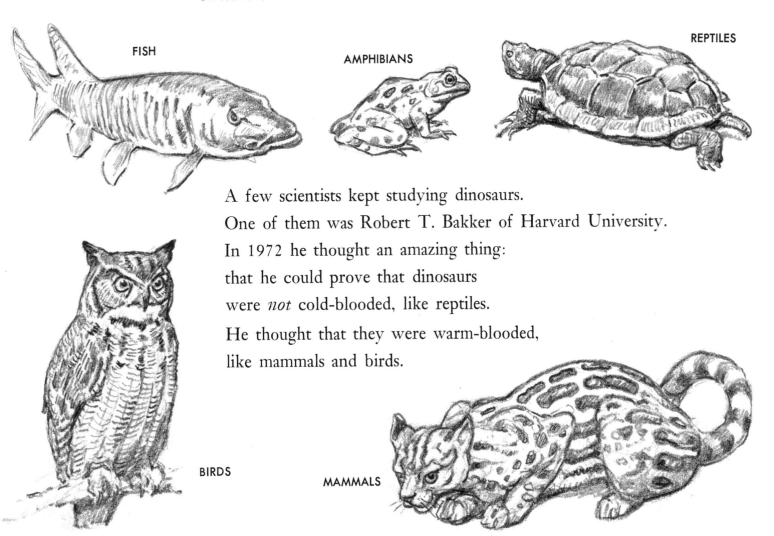

CLASSES OF COLD-BLOODED ANIMALS (ECTOTHERMS)

FISH

AMPHIBIANS

REPTILES

A few scientists kept studying dinosaurs.
One of them was Robert T. Bakker of Harvard University.
In 1972 he thought an amazing thing:
that he could prove that dinosaurs
were *not* cold-blooded, like reptiles.
He thought that they were warm-blooded,
like mammals and birds.

BIRDS

MAMMALS

CLASSES OF WARM-BLOODED ANIMALS (ENDOTHERMS)

13

TURTLES

REPTILE GROUPS OF TODAY

Was it possible?
If dinosaurs were warm-blooded,
then they weren't really reptiles.
And for a hundred years scientists had said
that dinosaurs were reptiles.

All of the reptiles we know
are cold-blooded.

SNAKES

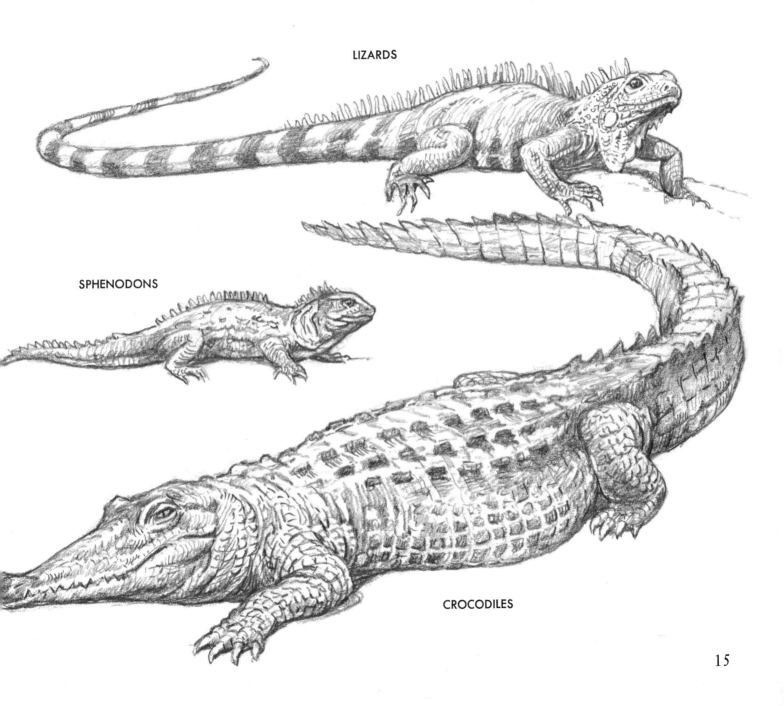

LIZARDS

SPHENODONS

CROCODILES

15

A cold-blooded animal—such as an alligator—
doesn't really have "cold" blood.
Its blood, and the rest of its body,
are about as cold or as warm as
the air or water around it.
The alligator can get warmer
by basking in the sun.

ALLIGATOR IN WARM SUN
Body temperature 35 degrees C (95 degrees F)
Air temperature 26 degrees C (80 degrees F)

16

The alligator can't stay in the sun for too long.
It will overheat and die.
So it cools off in the water, or in the shade.
It can't stay in the cool water too long, either.
Its body doesn't work well if it gets too cool.
So it goes in and out of the water.

ALLIGATOR IN COOL RIVER
Body temperature 29 degrees C (85 degrees F)
Water temperature 16 degrees C (60 degrees F)

17

A large reptile takes much longer
to warm up than a small reptile does,
just as a large pan of water
take longer to warm up than a small pan.
A large reptile keeps its body heat longer, too.
But it can't help cooling off
at night when the sun is gone.

MARINE IGUANA, A LIZARD
OF THE GALÁPAGOS ISLANDS

Small reptiles can live in places with cold winters.
When winter comes, they move more and more slowly.
Finally they get so cool they can't move at all.
They sleep deeply. This sleep is called hibernation.

A TURTLE UNDER
THE MUD OF A POND

RATTLESNAKES IN A
ROCKY WINTER BURROW

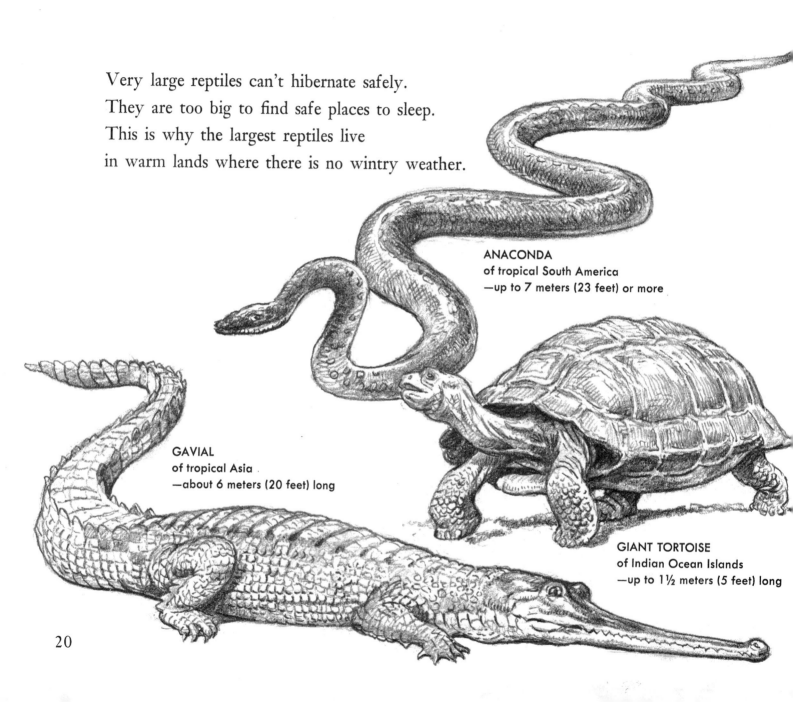

Very large reptiles can't hibernate safely.
They are too big to find safe places to sleep.
This is why the largest reptiles live
in warm lands where there is no wintry weather.

ANACONDA
of tropical South America
—up to 7 meters (23 feet) or more

GAVIAL
of tropical Asia
—about 6 meters (20 feet) long

GIANT TORTOISE
of Indian Ocean Islands
—up to 1½ meters (5 feet) long

20

When spring comes, the air warms.
Small reptiles warm up, too.
They wake up and go about their lives.
But they can't move about until their bodies are quite warm.
This is why we often see reptiles basking in the sun.

GREEN ANOLE

SOUTHERN PAINTED TURTLE

EASTERN KINGSNAKE

Large modern reptiles are all sluggish.
They can move quickly, but only for a very short time.
Then they must rest.
Their cold-blooded bodies don't work
as well as warm-blooded bodies.

A KOMODO DRAGON LIZARD RUNS QUICKLY
FOR SHORT DISTANCES TO CATCH A PIG

A WARM-BLOODED TIGER CAN
RUN SWIFTLY FOR A MUCH LONGER TIME

Dr. Bakker asked himself some questions about dinosaurs:

Did they have bodies like modern reptiles?

Did they act like modern reptiles?

Did they live in warm places only?

If the answer was "Yes,"

then dinosaurs really were cold-blooded reptiles.

TRACHODON,
A DUCK-BILLED DINOSAUR

23

Dr. Bakker studied many dinosaurs.

This one was about 2½ meters (8 feet) long.

It had large muscles in its hind legs.

It was built for running. *Fast!*

(It probably could go 64 kilometers [40 miles] an hour.)

But Dr. Bakker said that

a cold-blooded animal wouldn't have enough energy

to power those big leg muscles.

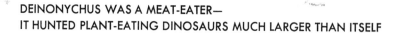

DEINONYCHUS WAS A MEAT-EATER—
IT HUNTED PLANT-EATING DINOSAURS MUCH LARGER THAN ITSELF

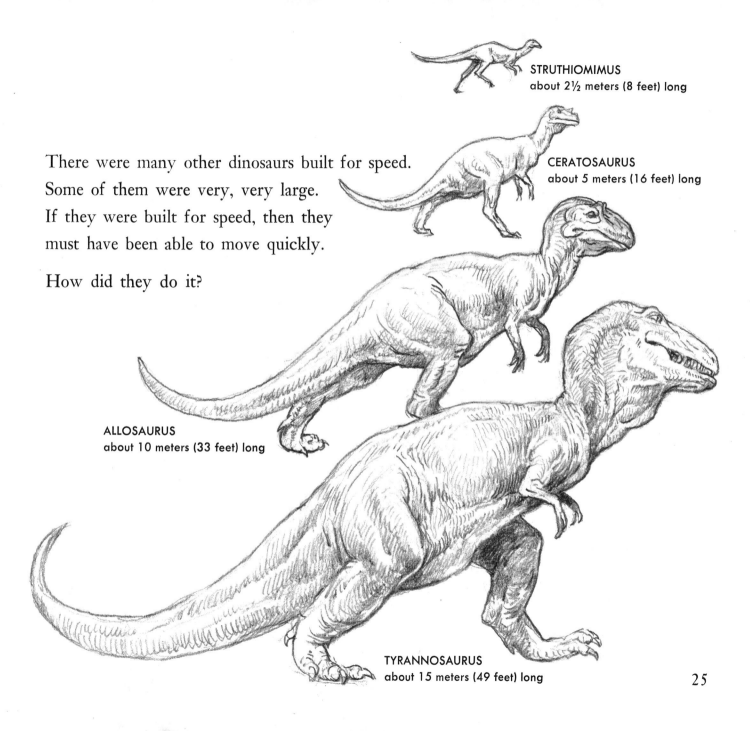

There were many other dinosaurs built for speed. Some of them were very, very large. If they were built for speed, then they must have been able to move quickly.

How did they do it?

STRUTHIOMIMUS
about 2½ meters (8 feet) long

CERATOSAURUS
about 5 meters (16 feet) long

ALLOSAURUS
about 10 meters (33 feet) long

TYRANNOSAURUS
about 15 meters (49 feet) long

Huge dinosaurs fought each other.
(We can see fossil bones with teeth marks.)
But fighting takes a lot of energy.
The bigger the fighters, the more energy is needed.
Dr. Bakker studied the energy that would be needed
for large dinosaurs to run fast and fight hard.

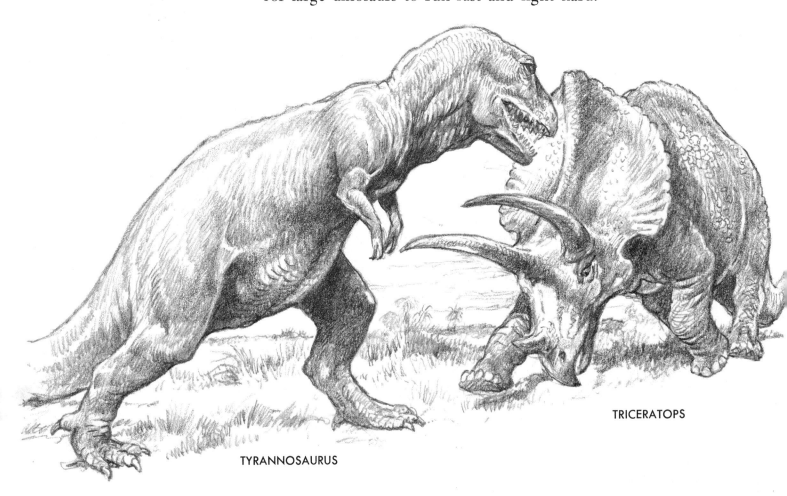

TRICERATOPS

TYRANNOSAURUS

He decided that cold-blooded bodies wouldn't
be able to run and fight for very long.
He said that the only kind of body
that would give them enough energy
would be a warm-blooded body.

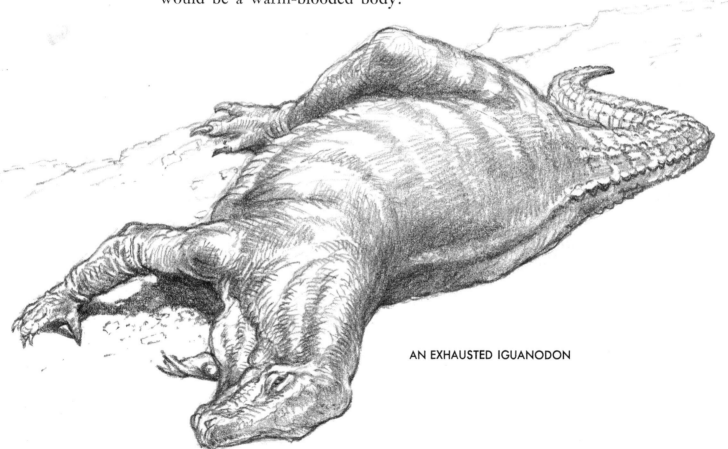

AN EXHAUSTED IGUANODON

Did any dinosaurs live in cold places?
Canadian scientists found some that did.
They were as big as a rhinoceros.
But large *cold-blooded* dinosaurs
could not survive outside the tropics.
Only *warm-blooded* dinosaurs could.

HYPACROSAURUS, A DUCK-BILLED
DINOSAUR THAT LIVED IN CANADA

Did dinosaurs have bodies like modern reptiles?
All that is left of dinosaurs is their bones.
But bones can tell a lot.
Warm-blooded animals have bones with
many holes for blood vessels.
Cold-blooded animals have bones
with only a few blood-vessel holes.
Dr. Bakker studied dinosaur bones.
They had many holes for blood vessels.

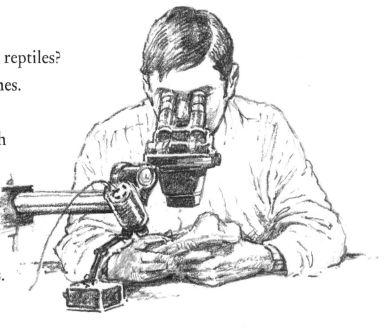

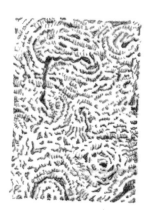

SLICE OF BONE FROM A
WARM-BLOODED ANIMAL,
A HUMAN BEING

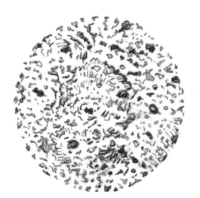

SLICE OF BONE FROM A
WARM-BLOODED ANIMAL,
AN OSTRICH

SLICE OF BONE FROM A
COLD-BLOODED ANIMAL,
PTERODACTYL,
AN EXTINCT REPTILE

Dr. Bakker answered his own questions.

Did dinosaurs have bodies like modern reptiles?

No.

Did they act like modern reptiles?

No.

Did they live in warm places only?

No.

He told the world of science
that dinosaurs were warm-blooded.
And many scientists believed him.

A new door opened in the study of dinosaurs.

If they were warm-blooded, then . . .

they weren't sluggish monsters.

They could be active in cool weather as well as in warm.

BRACHIOSAURUS WAS ONCE THOUGHT TO BE
TOO WEAK TO LIVE OUTSIDE WATER
THAT COULD HOLD UP ITS HUGE BODY

Big dinosaurs wouldn't have to waste time
basking in the sun for days and days
just to get their bodies warm enough to work.

WARM-BLOODED BRACHIOSAURUS
COULD EASILY HAVE WALKED ON LAND
AS WELL AS SWUM IN WATER

And maybe some dinosaurs even had fur or feathers.
Warm-blooded animals that live
in very hot or very cold places
need fur or feathers.
Their coats keep them
from getting too cold or too hot.

FENNEC FOX

AFRICAN DESERT CAT

QUAIL

DESERT ANIMALS MUST BE ABLE
TO STAND COLD NIGHTS AND HOT DAYS

Small warm-blooded animals
lose body heat faster than large animals.
It would be very important for
small dinosaurs to have some kind of coat.

DR. BAKKER SHOWED THIS SMALL
SYNTARSUS DINOSAUR WITH FEATHERY SCALES

SORDUS, THE "HAIRY DEVIL," WAS A PTEROSAUR,
A WARM-BLOODED CLOSE RELATIVE OF DINOSAURS.
ITS FOSSIL WAS FOUND IN RUSSIA

So far, scientists have not found
dinosaur fossils that show fur or feathers.
But these things are rarely seen as fossils.
The fossils of this close relative of dinosaurs
did show a furry coat very clearly.

For years, scientists knew that some small dinosaurs
had skeletons much like those of primitive birds.
The Archaeopteryx fossil showed feathers.
But if it hadn't,
scientists would have thought it was a dinosaur.

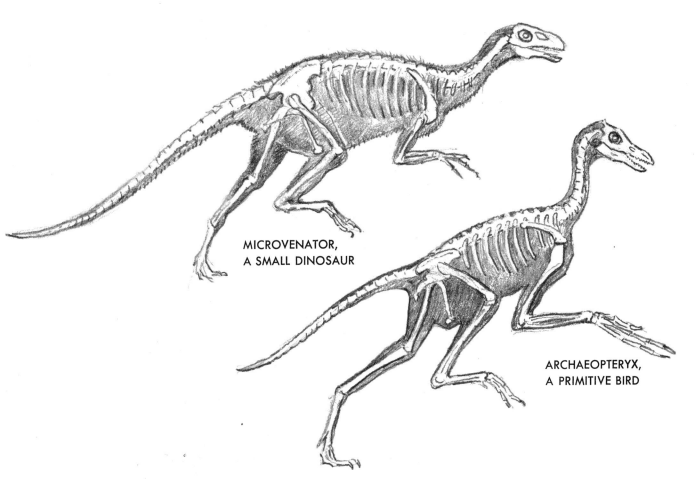

MICROVENATOR,
A SMALL DINOSAUR

ARCHAEOPTERYX,
A PRIMITIVE BIRD

Scientists have believed for a long time
that birds and reptiles had a common ancestor.
But they also thought that birds
were the first warm-blooded animals.

STEGOCERAS,
A "DOME-HEADED" DINOSAUR

BIRDS AND DINOSAURS LIVED TOGETHER 70 MILLION YEARS AGO

ICHTHYORNIS,
A TOOTHED, FLYING BIRD

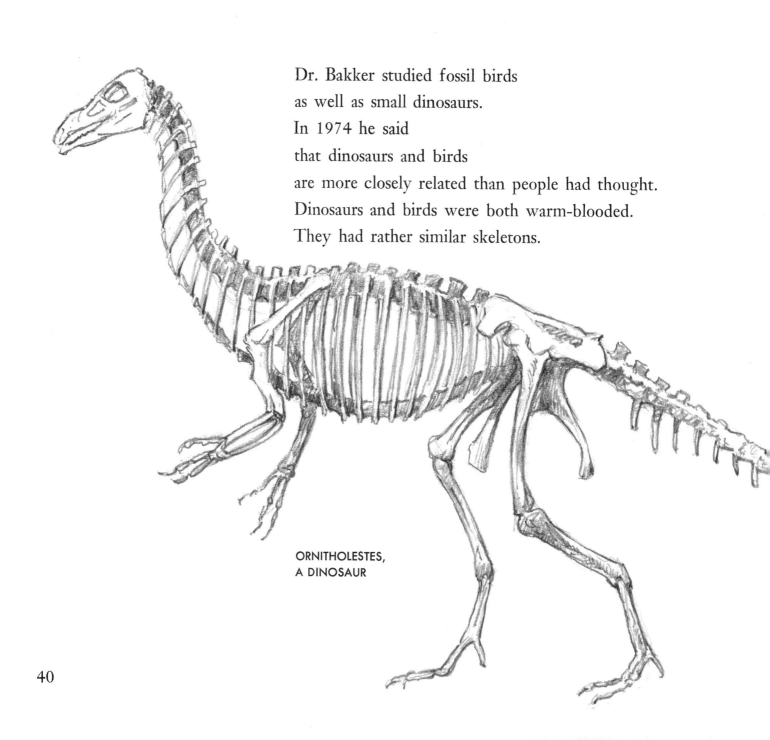

Dr. Bakker studied fossil birds
as well as small dinosaurs.
In 1974 he said
that dinosaurs and birds
are more closely related than people had thought.
Dinosaurs and birds were both warm-blooded.
They had rather similar skeletons.

ORNITHOLESTES,
A DINOSAUR

DOMESTIC FOWL,
A CHICKEN

41

Dr. Bakker drew a new family tree
for animals with backbones.
Compare it with the old family tree
on page 11.
Look carefully at the dinosaur "branch."

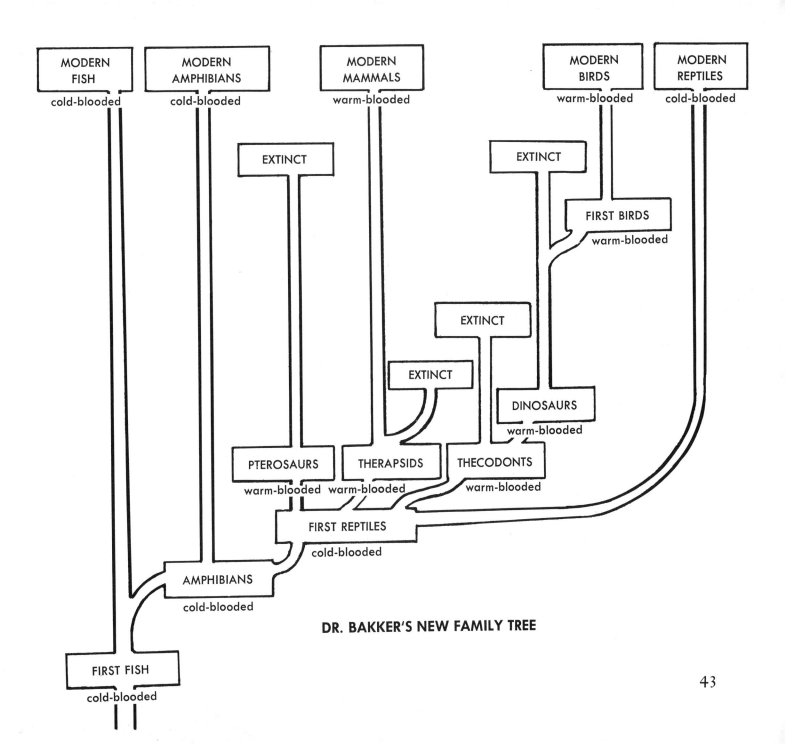

DR. BAKKER'S NEW FAMILY TREE

43

Dr. Bakker's family tree is so new
that other scientists are still studying it.

But if it is true,

then the dinosaurs did *not* all die sixty million years ago.

Their close relatives are all around us today.

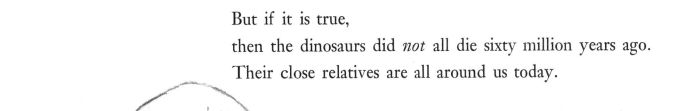

Their warm-blooded bodies are covered with feathers.
Their legs have scales.
Their bones have holes for blood vessels,
much like dinosaur bones.
We have been seeing "living dinosaurs"
almost every day, without knowing it—
but we call them birds.

INDEX